LET'S GET ZAPPING...

SO WHAT SHOULD YOU BE ZAPPING IN THE ANNUAL?

Wherever you see the **interactive icon** you'll be able to unlock a fun experience to enjoy on your device. There are 15 scattered throughout the book to discover.

See if you can find them all.

KT-434-537

READY.

Open Zappar on your device and find the Zapcode in the menu.

AIM.

Tap the Zapcode icon in the menu and scan the code on the page to download the content to your device.

ZAP.

Then point your device at the page and watch it come to life.

A FEW HELPFUL TIPS...

To get the best possible experience here are a few hints and tips:

- Connect to wifi if you can and the experiences will download even quicker than on 3G.

- Try and keep the pages as flat as you can for the best effect. Rest the book on a table or on the floor.

- Try and keep the full page in view from your phone after scanning the code. Don't get too close or far away if you can help it.

- Try and keep the pages clean and free from tears, pen and other marks as this may affect the experience.

- It's best to view the pages in good lighting conditions if you can.

If you're still having problems then do contact us at **support@zappar.com** and we'll do our best to help you.

CONTENTS PAGE

◆ Unlock bonus interactive features!

Published 2013. Pedigree Books Limited, Beech Hill
House, Walnut Gardens, Exeter, Devon EX4 4DH.
www.pedigreebooks.com – books@pedigreegroup.co.uk
The Pedigree trademark, email and website addresses,
are the sole and exclusive properties of Pedigree Group
Limited, used under licence in this publication.

ROVIO
BOOKS

LUCAS
BOOKS

Pedigree®

ANGRY BIRDS™
STAR WARS™

Round about snacktime in a galaxy far, far away, a few Bird Rebels have got their feathers in a flap.

Not only has the emperor banned all sweets, but he also believes that the Bird Rebels are hiding a mysterious and all-powerful Egg.

The Egg holds the power to rule the galaxy, and the emperor's evil henchpig Lard Vader is longing to get his trotters on it.

The Bird Rebels don't know why they are being treated like outlaws, and they don't know where to find The Egg. But they do know that emperor Piglatine's oink-brained Pigtroopers won't leave them alone, and they've had enough.

It's time to get...
ANGRY!

RED SKYWALKER

LIGHTSABER

JEDI POUCH

FREE INTERACTIVE PROFILE PAGE
ZAP THIS PAGE TO UNLOCK

UTILITY BELT

GENDER: Male
LOYALTY: Bird Rebels
WEAPON: Lightsaber
STRENGTH: Medium
POWERS: Using a lightsaber
LIKES: Fighting Pigtroopers with his lightsaber
HATES: Lard Vader

Hot-headed Red Skywalker thinks he knows everything, but he's got a lot to learn. He's good-hearted but clumsy, and he's way too impatient. He can't wait to find The Egg and discover its secrets. Will his Jedi training be completed in time to defeat Lard Vader and the Pigtroopers?

PRINCESS STELLA ORGANA

ROYAL HAIRSTYLE

DETERMINED EYES

HIDDEN BLASTER

GENDER: Female
LOYALTY: Bird Rebels
WEAPON: Blaster
STRENGTH: Medium
POWERS: Using a blaster as a tractor beam
LIKES: Being in charge
HATES: Being ignored

This dramatic Princess only cares about one thing – freeing her home planet from the clutches of the Emperor. She is one of the leaders of the Bird Rebellion, and even her friends admit that she's bossy. But she's brave and honest, with a bit of a soft spot for Ham Solo!

YODA BIRD

WRINKLES OF WISDOM

GOOD LISTENER

POWERFUL LIGHTSABER

GENDER: Male
LOYALTY: Jedi
WEAPON: The Force
STRENGTH: Very strong
POWERS: Extremely agile with a lightsaber
LIKES: Talking backwards
HATES: Forgetting things

Yoda Bird is wise, patient . . . and forgetful. This old Jedi Master was the one who hid The Egg in the first place. But for how long can he remember where he put it? He wants to share the secret with Red, but the young Jedi isn't ready for the responsibility.

OBI-WAN KABOOMI

THOUGHTFUL
EXPRESSION

JEDI ROBE

SIMPLE CLOTHING

GENDER:	Male
LOYALTY:	Jedi
WEAPON:	The Force
STRENGTH:	Strong
POWERS:	Levitating objects
LIKES:	Big explosions
HATES:	Failed explosions

Jedi warrior Obi-Wan Kaboomi loves using the Force to make BIG explosions. The trouble is, he's not always very good at controlling them. He's longing to use his powers to protect The Egg, but he has no idea where to find it.

R2-EGG2

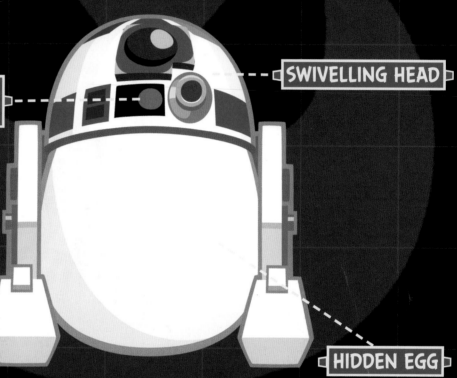

COMMUNICATING DEVICE

SWIVELLING HEAD

HIDDEN EGG

GENDER: Male
LOYALTY: Bird Rebels
WEAPON: Electrifying beam
STRENGTH: Medium
POWERS: Electrifying
LIKES: Helping out his friends
HATES: Being left out

Cheeky R2-EGG2 is a brave little droid who is always ready for adventure. But there's much more to this machine than meets the eye. Much more than just a droid, R2-EGG2 is actually a very cunning disguise for The Egg itself!

C-3PYOLK

OBEDIENT STARE

WORRIED SMILE

SHINY GOLD CASING

GENDER: Male
LOYALTY: Bird Rebels
WEAPON: None
STRENGTH: Weak
POWERS: Splitting into
five pieces
LIKES: Obeying
orders
HATES: Being in danger

Protocol droid, interpreter and peacemaker – C-3PYOLK has many roles and is always trying to find diplomatic solutions. Between worrying about the future, taking care of plants and working for the Bird Rebels, C-3PYOLK's job is never done!

TEREBACCA

FIERCE EXPRESSION

RAZOR-SHARP TEETH

TOOL BELT

GENDER: Male
LOYALTY: Ham Solo
WEAPON: Teeth
STRENGTH: Super Strong
POWERS: Causing earthquakes
LIKES: Ham Solo
HATES: Danger

Ham Solo's co-pilot and mechanic is just a great big grunting ball of feathers, and Ham is the only one who understands him. Terebacca is a skilled mechanic, which makes him very useful to the Bird Rebels – even if they are a bit scared of him!

CHUCK 'HAM' SOLO

UNRULY HAIR

BLASTER

COCKY EXPRESSION

GENDER:	Male
LOYALTY:	Terebacca
WEAPON:	Blaster
STRENGTH:	Medium
POWERS:	Three shots in blaster
LIKES:	Smuggling
HATES:	Getting caught

A famous food smuggler, a skilled pilot and a charming scoundrel – Ham Solo can turn his hand to anything. He seems confident, but most of the time he doesn't have a clue what he's doing. Ham owes money to crooks around the universe, but somehow he always manages to keep one step ahead of them!

LARD VADER

PIG-SHAPED HELMET

TRUE FACE HIDDEN

VOICE BOX

Once a Jedi warrior, now the Emperor's right-hand pig, Lard Vader has a sense of ambition as big as the galaxy. He is sure that if he can only find The Egg, he will become ruler of the universe.

GENDER:	Male
LOYALTY:	Pig Empire
WEAPON:	The Force
STRENGTH:	Strong
POWERS:	Levitating objects
LIKES:	Scaring the the Bird Rebels
HATES:	Weakness

EMPEROR PIGLATINE

FACE TOO HIDEOUS TO BE SEEN

LARGE NOSTRILS FOR SNIFFING OUT ENEMIES

MOUTH OPEN FOR CANDY

FREE INTERACTIVE PROFILE PAGE
ZAP THIS PAGE TO UNLOCK

The ruler of the Pig Empire is so greedy that he wants to eat all the junk food in the universe. He has banned candy and junk food for everyone except himself. In fact, he's so busy thinking about eating, he hasn't realised that Lard Vader wants to take his place as leader!

GENDER:	Male
LOYALTY:	Pig Empire
WEAPON:	The Pig Star
STRENGTH:	Very strong
POWERS:	Brainwash
LIKES:	Candy and sweet treats
HATES:	Bird Rebels

CODE RED!

Red Skywalker is setting off on a secret mission! Use your colouring pens to complete this exciting scene.

MEMORY LANE

Set a timer and look carefully at this picture for 60 seconds. Try to remember every little detail, then cover the picture and answer the questions below.

I. Is Obi-Wan Kaboomi in the picture?

....

2. On which side of the image are the Bird Rebels?

....

3. What image is on the computer screen?

....

7. What colour is the planet?

....

8. Who has one eye closed?

....

9. What has the Emperor been eating?

....

Yoda Bird is getting forgetful, so he wants to find out about your memory. Is it as full of holes as Lard Vader's helmet or razor sharp like Terebacca's teeth? You can find out by taking this quickfire test.

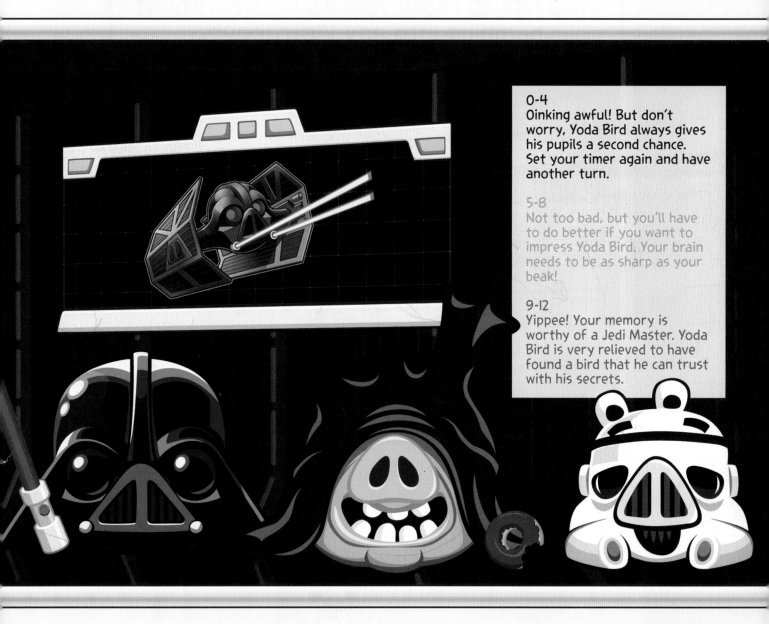

0-4
Oinking awful! But don't worry, Yoda Bird always gives his pupils a second chance. Set your timer again and have another turn.

5-8
Not too bad, but you'll have to do better if you want to impress Yoda Bird. Your brain needs to be as sharp as your beak!

9-12
Yippee! Your memory is worthy of a Jedi Master. Yoda Bird is very relieved to have found a bird that he can trust with his secrets.

4. Who is standing next to Red Skywalker?

....

5. How many Pigtroopers are in the picture?

....

6. Whose lightsaber has been turned on?

....

10. How many TIE fighters are there?

....

11. Which side of the picture is the computer screen on?

....

12. Is Emperor Piglatine's mouth closed?

....

MAZE MUDDLE

Ham Solo needs to deliver his smuggled candy cargo to Jabba the Hog. Can you help him to reach Jabba's castle without bumping into any Pigtroopers?

FINISH!

RESCUING THE PRINCESS

There's a lot of anger in space.

The Pigtroopers won't leave the birds alone, and the birds have had enough.

A group of especially angry Bird Rebels have stolen the plans to Emperor Piglatine's new weapon, the Pig Star. He's oinking furious! When they find its weakest spots, they'll be able to blow it to pieces.

Princess Stella Organa is angry too. It's her job to deliver the plans to the Bird Rebels, but Lard Vader and his Pigtroopers have captured her ship.

"Take these plans to Obi-Wan Kaboomi," she tells R2-EGG2.

"We need his help to find The Egg and defeat the Pig Empire!"

Lard Vader captures the Princess, but he can't find the plans. Can she escape before he splats her like an egg? She curls her beak and glares at him.

"I'm not scared of you!" she says.

"You will be!" hisses Lard Vader.

"Where are those plans? And where's The Egg?"

AN UGLY CRIME LORD FROM RED'S HOME PLANET HAS BEEN MAKING FAKE EGGS TO CONFUSE THE BIRD REBELS. FIND ALL THE FAKE EGGS AND THEN SCRAMBLE THEM TO DISCOVER THE NAME OF THE CRIME LORD!

R2-EGG2 and C-3PYOLK hurtle away from the ship in an escape pod.

"WE'RE DOOMED!"

C-3PYOLK wails as they plunge through space.

R2-EGG2 chirrups. He has a difficult mission, but he's ready for anything. If he can just survive the crash landing . . .

The escape pod crashes on a hot, sandy planet, and the droids are promptly captured by some Jawa Birds. These traders sell R2-EGG2 and C-3PYOLK to a young farmer called Red Skywalker.

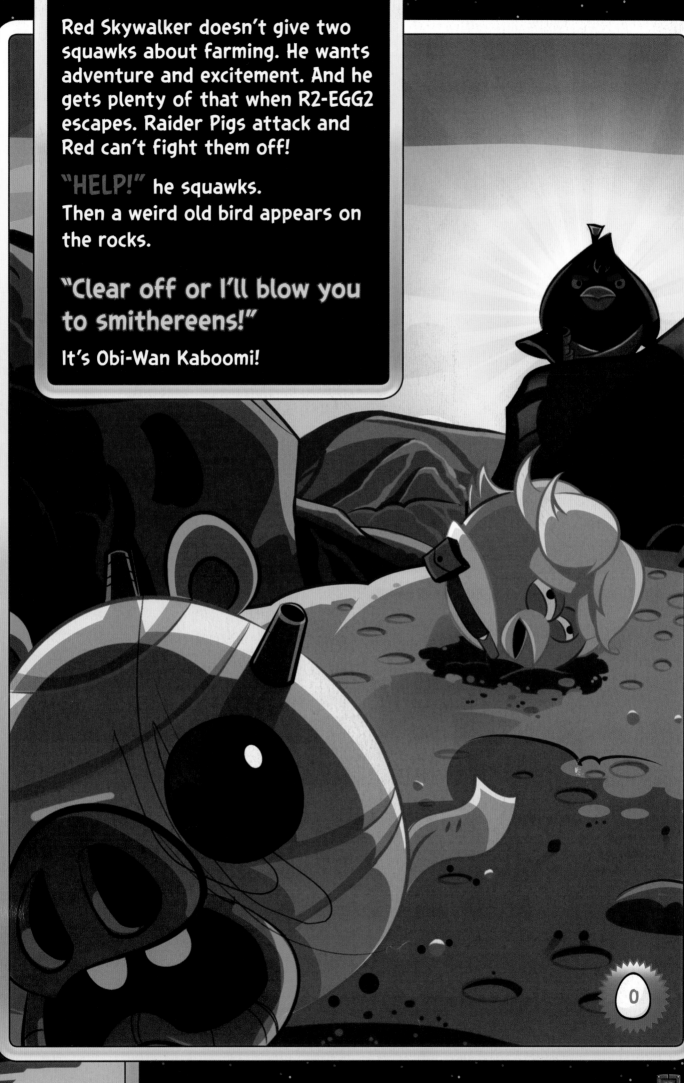

Red Skywalker doesn't give two squawks about farming. He wants adventure and excitement. And he gets plenty of that when R2-EGG2 escapes. Raider Pigs attack and Red can't fight them off!

"HELP!" he squawks.
Then a weird old bird appears on the rocks.

"Clear off or I'll blow you to smithereens!"

It's Obi-Wan Kaboomi!

0

In Obi-Wan's cave, Red hears amazing news.

"I knew your father, Red,"

says Obi-Wan.

"He was the best flyer in the galaxy!"

He gives Red a sword made of pure energy.

"That's a lightsaber, and it once belonged to your father," he says.

"This is SO COOL!"

squawks Red.

He swishes it through the air and sets fire to the carpet.

"Patience, young one," said Obi-Wan, blowing out a flame on his hood.

"Use the Force and focus on what's really important . . . FINDING THE EGG!"

Obi-Wan Kaboomi takes Red to a cantina in the dangerous part of town.

"I've never been anywhere like this before,"

says Red. "Who's that? What are they drinking? Why is he so hairy? What's that smell?"

"Watch your beak, kid,"

says the yellow stranger. "Stay cool."

"This is Chuck 'Ham' Solo and Terebacca," says Obi-Wan.

"They're going to fly us out of here to join the Bird Rebels!"

TO BE CONTINUED...ON PAGE 50

TO BE CONTINUED...ON PAGE 50

THE UGLY CRIME LORD IS...

BIRD BOUNTY

Lard Vader has lost his temper and put a price on the head of his enemies! He has given the bounty hunters these photos to help them track down their victims. Can you identify each one so that the Bird Rebels can warn them?

COUNT THE EGGS

The Emperor has been searching for The Egg all over the galaxy, and he has found plenty of fakes along the way. How many eggs can you spot?

"I can see .... eggs."

EGG'S THE WORD

FIGHT
ATOOINEG
GALAXYODA
BIRDROIDSTAR
SHIPIGTROOP
ERSMUGGLER
EBELIGHTSAB
EREPUBLIC

Can you figure out the words that complete this Egg-shaped puzzle? Each answer begins with the last letter of the previous answer.

1. Red Skywalker's home planet.................................
2. Something Lard Vader wants to find.................
3. The star system...
4. An elderly Jedi Master..
5. C-3PYOLK and R2-EGG2 are both........................
6. The *Mighty Falcon* is a.......................................
7. The Emperor's minions..
8. Ham Solo's illegal job..
9. Princess Stella is a secret Bird..........................
10. The weapon of a Jedi..

ANGRY PAIRS

These furious fighters have lost their weapons!
Can you match each one to the correct weapon?

1. Hog Guard

2. 'Ham' Solo

3. Ewok Bird

4. Obi-Wan

5. Lard Vader

A. Blaster

B. Blue Lightsaber

C. Fork

D. Red Lightsaber

E. Catapult

PAPER PLANET

Now you can become more powerful than Emperor Piglantine himself and create your own galaxy – one planet at a time! Follow these simple steps to make a world out of papier mâché.

You will need:
White flour
Water
Newspaper
Balloon
String
Paintbrushes
Paint
Pin

MY PLANET IS CALLED...

ALERT!
Always ask for help from an adult when using scissors.

1. Blow up your balloon and put a knot in the neck. Tie a piece of string around the knot.

2. Tear the newspaper into long, thin strips.

3. Mix one part flour with one part water. (You can experiment with these amounts to make the mixture thinner or thicker.)

4. Stir the mixture until it is smooth.

5. Dip a strip of newspaper into the mixture, and then lay it over the surface of the balloon. Make it as smooth as you can.

6. Keep putting strips on the balloon until it is covered. You will need at least two layers, but no more than four.

7. Hang the balloon up to dry and harden. (This is where you will need the patience of a Jedi Master. You might have to wait overnight. Spend the time thinking about what colours to paint your planet.)

8. Paint the balloon and hang it up to dry.

9. Finally, stick the pin through the papier mâché to pop the balloon. (Wear a thimble to protect your fingers and ask an adult for help.)

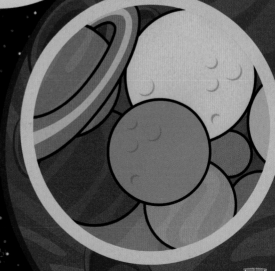

JIGSAW JUMBLE

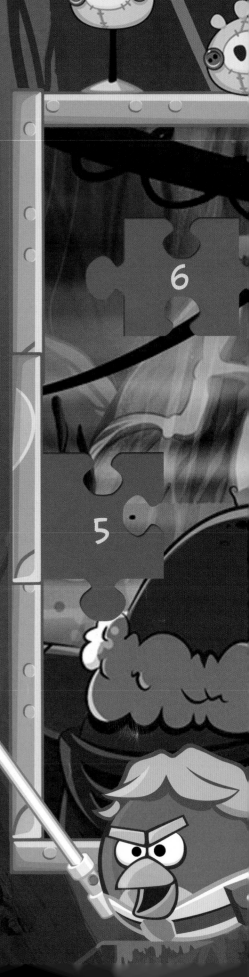

Yoda Bird is so forgetful that he can't remember how to complete this jigsaw. Can you help him? Match the jigsaw shapes to the spaces in the picture.

A

B

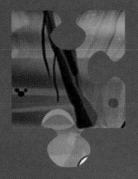

C

D

E

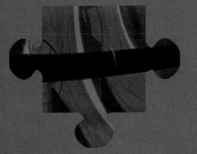

F

PIGSTY PALACE

JUNK FOOD

TNT

JUNK FOOD

Jabba the Hog's palace is a real pigsty! He has ordered C-3PYOLK to tidy up, but the poor protocol droid doesn't know where to start.

Can you see?

Doughnut..................
Lightsaber..................
Catapult..................
Box of dynamite......
Medal..................
Blaster..................

Boulder..................
Wooden plank..........
Vine..................
Bread..................
Sleeping Pigtrooper.
Jedi cloak..................
Utility belt..................

COLOUR BY NUMBERS

FREE INTERACTIVE ACTIVITY PAGE
ZAP THIS PAGE TO UNLOCK

JUNK DEFENDERS!

The Bird Rebels are attacking!

They know that the Pigtroopers on Tatooine are guarding a stash of junk food, and they want to take it back. Which angry Rebel will be the first to reach the food?

10 **11**

You hit a stone wall. Miss a turn.

13 **14**

You disable a Pig Walker. Next time you throw the dice, double the number you throw.

21 **22** **23** **24**

30 **31** **32** **33**

You knock down a tall tower. Have another turn.

40

You can see the food stash! Go forward three spaces.

42 **43** **44**

Equipment

Markers
Dice
Two or more players

How to Play

1. Choose a player to start the attack. Throw the dice and deploy your first Bird Rebel.
2. Follow any instructions you land on.
3. The winner is the first player to reach the Pigtroopers' food stash.

 **START**

 **1**

 **2**

 Your shot goes wide. Next time you throw the dice, halve the number you throw.

4

 **5**

 **6**

 You smash your first target. Go forward five spaces.

 **8**

9

 A Pigtrooper fires at you. Retreat four spaces and hide.

 **16**

 **17**

18

 **19**

 **25**

 **26**

 **27**

 You run out of ammunition. Go back two spaces.

29

 **35**

 You are outnumbered. Swap marker places with the player on your right.

37

38

39

 **45**

 **46**

 Your attack has failed. Go back to the start and try again.

48

 **FINISH**

SHADOW MATCH

SHADOW MATCH

FREE INTERACTIVE ACTIVITY PAGE

ZAP THIS PAGE TO UNLOCK

Lard Vader likes to keep things dark. It's hard to tell your friends and enemies apart when the lights go down! Can you identify who is lurking in the shadows?

C-3PYOLK   R2-EGG2   Boba Fatt

Mace Windu   Lando Birdissian   Ewok Bird

SECRET SQUAWKS

CREATE CAB
a

WRY DARK LEEKS
d

I WIN OAK BAMBOO
b

LOOK CHUM - CASH
e

CLEANSERS SPILT
c

BADDY OR I
f

The Bird Rebels send their messages in code to confuse the Pigtroopers. They even disguise their names. Are you clever enough to unscramble these words and find out who these messages are for?

BIRD BASE

1	2	3	4	5	6	7	8
T	O	A	A	B	F	T	B

Red Skywalker is in danger on the planet Hoth! He has transmitted information about his attacker to the Bird Rebels, but the picture has been scrambled. Can you put the pieces in the right order and find the name of Red's enemy?

The correct order for the numers is:

Red is being attacked by:

ANGRY BIRDS STAR WARS

RESCUING HAM SOLO

READY! AIM! TWANG!

While the Pigtroopers are searching for the missing droids, Ham and Terebacca hurtle away from the planet – straight into the tractor beam of the Emperor's Pig Star!

There's a lot of anger on board the ship.

"This is all your fault!"

Ham bellows at Red.

"DON'T blame me; you're the pilot!" Red yells.

Terebacca glowers and makes a scary growling noise in his throat.

"Oh, I say!" C-3PYOLK protests.

"Was that really necessary?"

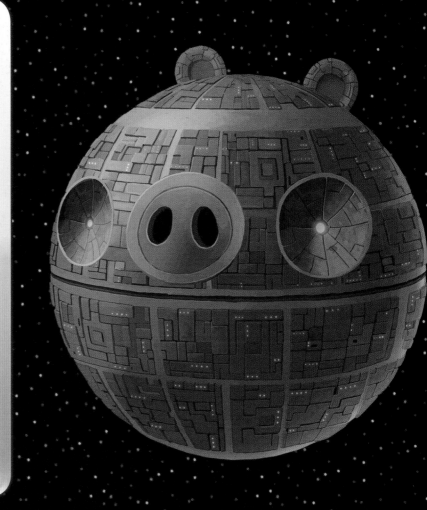

While everyone is blaming everyone else, the ship is dragged into the main hangar. Then R2-EGG2 chirrups some exciting news. Princess Stella is on board!

"**GOOD!**" shouts Red Skywalker, swinging his lightsaber around. "I **MUST** rescue her!"

"Let the Force of The Egg guide you,"

says Obi-Wan, ducking just in time to avoid **THE** blade.

After blasting a few Pigtroopers, Red Skywalker and Ham rescue Princess Stella.

"You took your time!" she snaps.

"Come on, let's get out of here!"

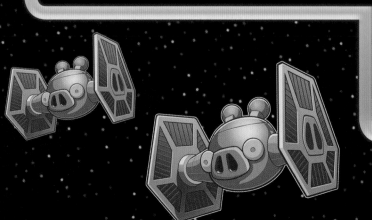

Meanwhile, Obi-Wan Kaboomi senses that his old pupil, Lard Vader, is on board. After checking the plans, he sets a massive bomb at the weakest point of the Pig Star, and then goes to pick a fight.

"I'll make your feathers fly!"

Snorts the **EVIL** Lard Vader.

"I'll smash you to smithereens!"

screeches Obi-Wan.

They fight an epic duel, but Obi-Wan Kaboomi has to sacrifice himself for his friends. There's only one thing to do.

He **LET**s Lard Vader **WIN**!

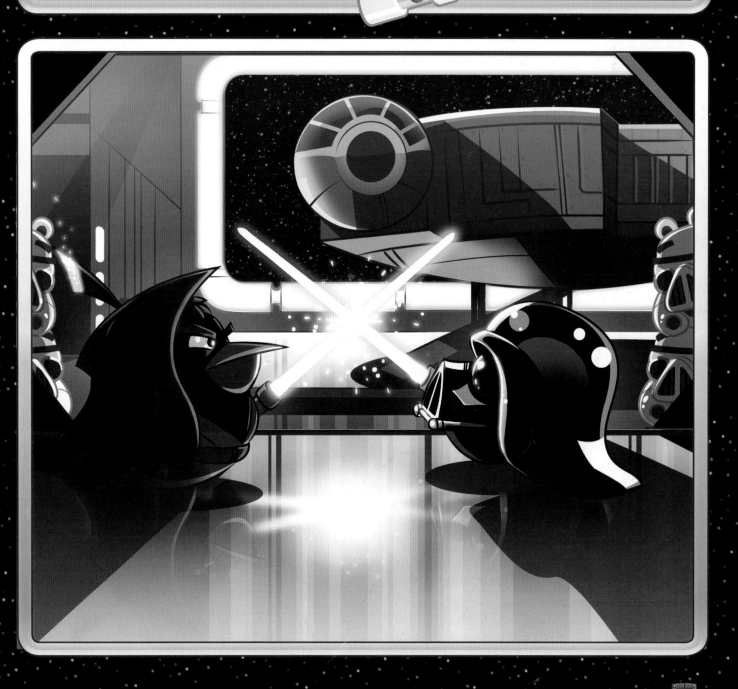

While Lard Vader is celebrating his **DEFEAT** of Obi-Wan, Red finds an awesome Birdfighter and jumps in.

"Now we'll see some serious flying action!"

he squawks in excitement.

"Look and learn, Ham!"

The ships rocket out of the Pig Star as Obi-Wan's bomb goes off.

KABOOM!

"Take that, **PORKERS!**" yells Red.

The explosion dazzles him, and he thinks that he hears the familiar voice of Obi-Wan Kaboomi.

"Stay true to the Force, Red!" he says.

"I will always be with you!"

There's a secret message in this story! Look for nine words in **BOLD** and then mix them up to discover your secret message.

THE END...

THE SECRET MESSAGE IS...

FREE INTERACTIVE STORY PAGE

ZAP THIS PAGE TO UNLOCK

IMAGINE THAT!

Have you ever made up your own stories? This is your chance to send your favourite characters on an exciting new adventure. These pages have been designed especially for you to make a brand-new comic strip. Fire up your imagination!

On a small, red planet far from home . . . .

FEELING CROSS?

This is the perfect puzzle for you if you're in a piggy temper!

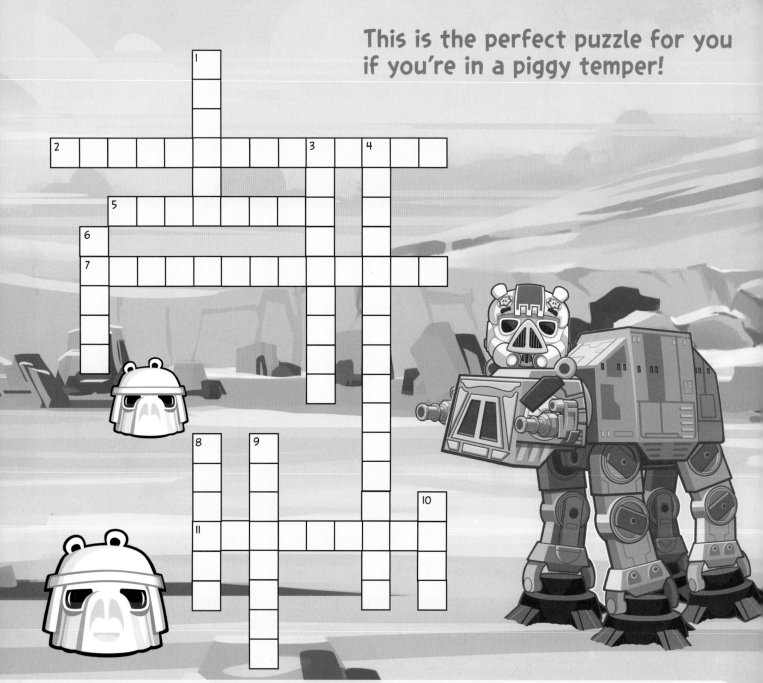

Down
1. Lard Vader is annoyed because he hasn't found this.
3. Name a pilot with a scary-sounding snarl.
4. A charming but crooked friend of Ham Solo's.
6. Something that the Jedi use to attack their enemies.
8. What do you lose when you get cross?
9. Something the Emperor likes eating.
10. Yoda Bird is a member of which order?

Across
2. Which sharp-beaked royal bird is always getting cross with Ham Solo?
5. Ham Solo is a well-known _____.
7. Who causes explosions when he gets angry?
11. What is the Emperor's name?

WORDSEARCH

Twelve words meaning 'angry' are hidden in this grid.
Can you keep your temper and find them all?

Annoyed	Fuming	Infuriated	Moody
Cross	Furious	Irate	Outraged
Enraged	Incensed	Livid	Wrathful

```
E A J M D I F B L K N O C P G R M A Q T
S M W Z B Y A V S W R E A J M D V K X S
N D O P E S C P E E I T E S U O I R U F
K I K O L C H F R T P M V A T I W C H H
D W N Q D T Y L S A U Q L N F N V A M T
E T P I T W V N V D Y O J V P H R Y D
T K J M L I C P E I N U D M L K A S L
A Y P D S R Y B U F M T E M D K N X Y F
I Q T G S T N J V W R Z U S F N T P I G
R O B U O U T R A G E D N W O Q U L N O
U D M W R V B D K N H T E Y D M L I R N
F H M A C H J V E W R L E U D H M V H I
N O Z S U Q X G L S I D M K C U Y I F P
I W L C P E J O B D N B C X F Z T D K A
R F Y S X V A I K Z T E L N N U L G Q S
O E N R A G E D Q H T E C Z T M L D O U
F S K L N F D M W B T P M N M J F W D G
B Y I O J X C K E T P I T Y I S A E L O
M L Q J W R O U L R X M L Z G Y T U M
J N V A T G U S W R L U F H T A R W V C
```

59

HOW TO DRAW
OBI-WAN KABOOMI

FOLLOW THESE SIMPLE STEPS AND LEARN HOW TO DRAW THIS EXPLOSIVE JEDI MASTER!

STEP 1

Use lines and circles to create Obi-Wan's shape and pose.

STEP 2

Fill out his features with light pencil lines.

STEP 3

Gradually add the detail of Obi-Wan's clothes and expression.

STEP 4

Complete your drawing with careful colour and sharp pencil lines.

Jabba the Hog has a job for Boba Fatt.
The crime lord wants revenge on Ham Solo!

*Use the grid to copy Jabba's secret meeting
with the bounty hunter.*

PROTECT THE PIG!

The Pigtroopers keep trying to build an unshakeable hiding place, but those pesky Bird Rebels just keep smashing them to smithereens. The Pigtroopers started building another fortress, but when they saw the Bird Rebels they gave up and ran away. Now the Emperor is on the warpath and he wants a piggy palace pronto! Can you build a stronghold that will keep his junk food safe?

USE THE FORCE, RED!

JUNK FOOD

DESIGN A VEHICLE

SCHEMATICS

Name.................................
....
Top Speed.........................
Weapons...........................
....
Engine...............................
Crew..................................
....

Red has crashed his starfighter again! Design a brand new starship for him, and be quick about it! Red doesn't have a lot of patience . . .

DROID FRIENDS!

R2-EGG2 and C-3PYOLK make a great team, but they don't always agree! C-3PYOLK thinks that these pictures look exactly the same, but R2-EGG2 says that there are ten differences between them. Can you prove who is right by searching for the differences?

FREE INTERACTIVE ACTIVITY PAGE
ZAP THIS PAGE TO UNLOCK

DOODLE DRAMA

Who or what has made these Pigtroopers look so scared? Use a thick black felt tip and complete this trotter-trembling scene. Then colour in the picture.

MINIATURE MODEL

Bring the fight for the galaxy into your own room! Create a real-life space scene using ordinary items you can find around the house.

You will need:

Shoe box
Thick card
Paper
Paintbrushes
Paints
Glue
Glitter
Scissors
Crayons
Sticky tape
Sewing thread
Sand
Grey tissue paper

ALERT!
Always ask for help from an adult when using scissors.

1. Draw stars and planets on the paper and colour them with crayons or paints. Then cut them out.

2. Stand the box on one of the long sides and decorate the inside to look like outer space. Paint it black and stick on the stars and planets. Use your glitter to create a meteor shower!

3. Make the base of the box the surface of a planet. Paint glue onto the base and scatter sand onto it. You could also screw up grey tissue paper to make boulders.

4. Cut out the templates and stick them onto card, or copy your favourite characters onto card and colour them in. Then cut out the characters.

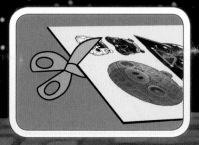

5. Hang the tiefighters and Pig Star from the roof of the box using tape and thread.

6. To finish, tape your characters to the bottom of the box.

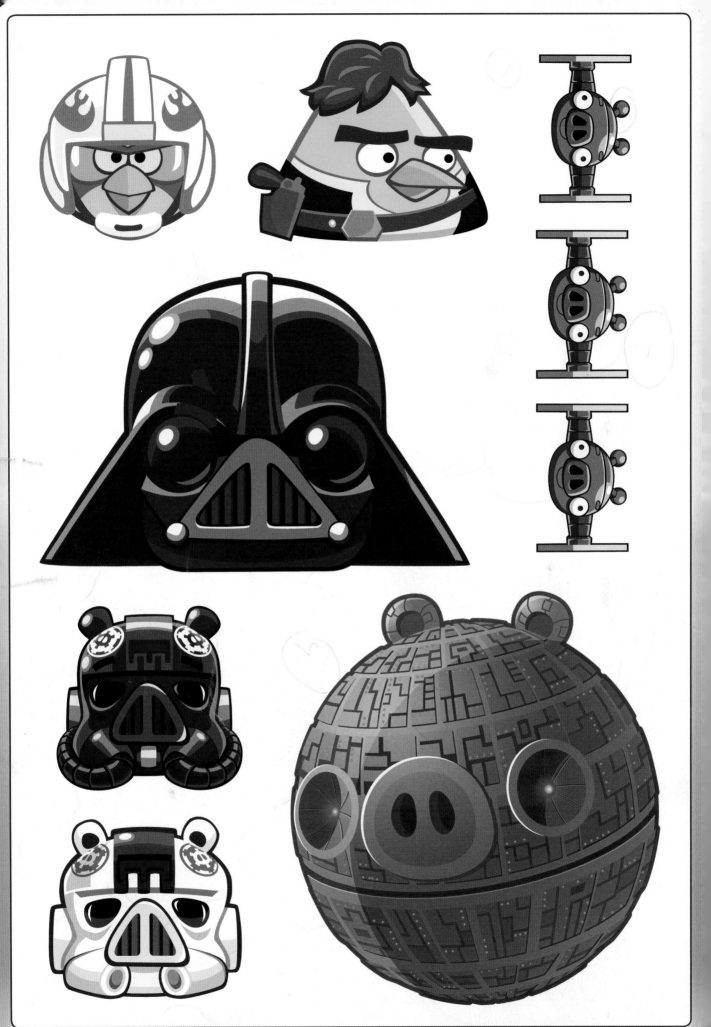

SPOT THE DIFFERENCE

While Obi-Wan and Lard Vader were fighting, some of the Pigtroopers stopped to capture the moment on camera. But there are five differences between these two snaps of the battle. Can you find them all?

SLIDE PUZZLE

BLUEPRINT SECTION..................

1

BLUEPRINT SECTION..................

2

BLUEPRINT SECTION..................

3

BLUEPRINT SECTION..................

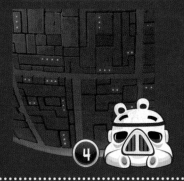

4

BLUEPRINT SECTION..................

5

BLUEPRINT SECTION..................

6

BLUEPRINT SECTION..................

7

BLUEPRINT SECTION..................

8

BLUEPRINT SECTION..................

9

These Pigtroopers are guarding nine sections of a very important picture. It is the blueprint of Emperor Piglatine's new Pig Star! Can you help the Bird Rebels by piecing together the blueprint? Figure out the correct order for the sections and write the numbers in the grid.

FREE INTERACTIVE ACTIVITY PAGE

ZAP THIS PAGE TO UNLOCK

INTERROGATION SQUAD!

Squawk! You've been captured by Lard Vader and he wants to find out how much you know. Your only hope is to give him the wrong answers!

The lower your score, the more likely it is that he will let you live.

1. Where is the Bird Rebel base?
   a. Hoth
   b. Jabba the Hog's palace

2. What does the Emperor do with junk food?
   a. Eats it
   b. Burns it

3. Who is Boba Fatt?
   a. A bounty hunter
   b. A shoe salespig

4. Why does Lard Vader want The Egg?
   a. To rule the galaxy
   b. To make an omelette

5. What side is Lard Vader on?
   a. The Pork Side
   b. Sunny side up

6. Who is this?
   a. Obi-Wan Kaboomi
   b. The local plumber

7. Name the droids who help the Bird Rebels.
   a. C-3PYOLK and R2-EGG2
   b. Grumpy and Chirpy

8. What power does the Blue Squadron have?
   a. The power of three
   b. The power of tea

9. What did this Bird Rebel help to steal?

   a. The blueprint of the Pig Star
   b. The Emperor's shopping list

10. What did Lard Vader used to be?
    a. Jedi Knight
    b. Cub scout

Mostly As

Oops! You just can't bear to be wrong, can you? Lard Vader is going to throw you in the Pig Star cells and throw away the key!

Mostly Bs

Congratulations! Your answers were pigthetic and Lard Vader thinks you're a fool. He is going to set you free!

Five of each

You should have tried harder to look like an idiot. Lard Vader is keeping you a prisoner and plans to question you again tomorrow!

PAGE 20-21

1. No
2. Left
3. Lard Vader's starfighter
4. Princess Stella
5. Three
6. Red Skywalker
7. Green
8. Red Skywalker
9. A doughnut
10. Five
11. Right
12. No

PAGE 22-23

PAGE 30

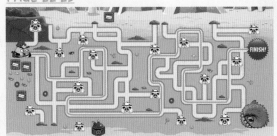

Red Skywalker   Princess Stella   Terebecca

Obi-Wan Kaboomi   Ham Solo   Mace Windu

PAGE 31

There are 16 eggs.

PAGE 32

TATOOINE
EGG
GALAXY
YODA BIRD
DROIDS
STARSHIP
PIGTROOPERS
SMUGGLER
REBEL
LIGHTSABER

PAGE 33

1-C, 2-A, ,3-E, 4-B, 5-D

PAGE 36-37

1-F, 2-D, 3-A, 4-E, 5-C, 6-B

PAGE 46-47

1. Lando Birdissian
2. R2-EGG2
3. Mace Windu
4. Boba Fatt
5. C-3PYOLK
6. Eok Bird

PAGE 48

a. Terebacca
b. Obi-Wan Kaboomi
c. Princess Stella
d. Red Skywalker
e. Chuck 'Ham' Solo
f. Yoda Bird

PAGE 49

8, 2, 5, 4, 6, 3, 7, 1
BOBA FATT

PAGE 58

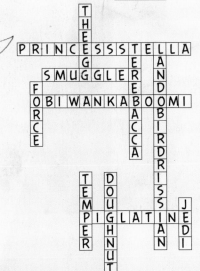

PAGE 59

PAGE 67

PAGE 72

PAGE 73

9,2,6,5,8,3,7,4,1

PAGE 74-75

1 - (a) Hoth
2 - (a) Eats it
3 - (a) A bounty hunter
4 - (a) To rule the galaxy
5 - (a) The Pork Side
6 - (a) Obi-Wan Kamoobi
7 - (a) C-3PYOLK and R2-EGG2
8 - (a) The power of three
9 - (a) The blueprint of the Pig Star
10 - (a) Jedi Knight

Angry Birds™ *Star Wars*™ Annual 2014

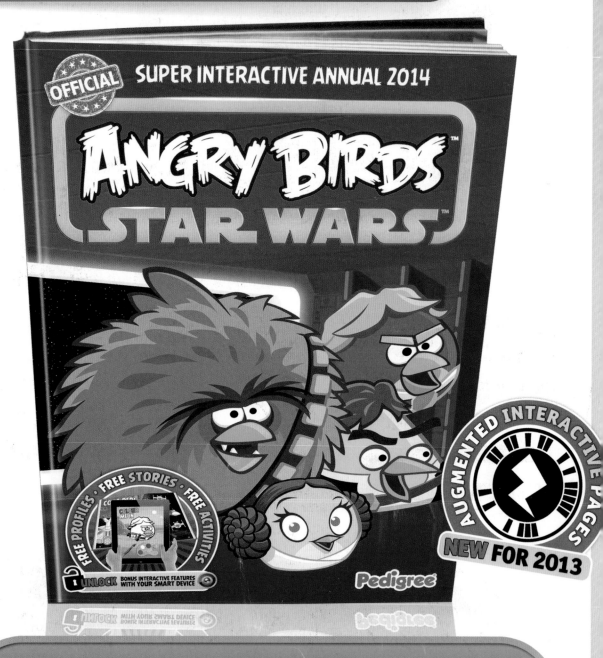

Visit **Pedigreebooks.com** to find out more on this year's **Angry Birds™ *Star Wars*™** Annual, scan with your mobile device to learn more.

Visit www.pedigreebooks.com

Pedigree Books, Beech Hill House, Walnut Gardens, Exeter EX4 4DH